ON HOLY GROUND

A BIBLE STUDY ON PRAYER

KIRKIE MORRISSEY

NAVPRESS

A MINISTRY OF THE NAVIGATORS
P.O. Box 6000, Colorado Springs, CO 80934

The Navigators is an international Christian organization.
Jesus Christ gave His followers the Great Commission to
go and make disciples (Matthew 28:19). The aim of The
Navigators is to help fulfill that commission by multiply-
ing laborers for Christ in every nation.

NavPress is the publishing ministry of The Navigators.
NavPress publications are tools to help Christians grow.
Although publications alone cannot make disciples or
change lives, they can help believers learn biblical disci-
pleship, and apply what they learn to their lives and
ministries.

Fifth printing, 1986

Scripture quotations are from the *Holy Bible: New International Version* (NIV). Copyright © 1973, 1978, 1984,
International Bible Society. Used by permission of Zondervan Bible Publishers.

Printed in the United States of America

Contents

To   Scott
Reid
Mark

the sons given to Terry and me as gifts from our
gracious heavenly Father.

For the joy each is
and for the love we share.

Author

Kirkie Morrissey coordinates women's Bible studies in Colorado Springs, Colorado. She also trains women to lead those studies. In addition to *On Holy Ground,* she has also written *In His Name* (NavPress), *Get Growin',* published by Young Life, *A Woman's Workshop on Forgiveness,* and *Designed by God,* the last two published by Zondervan Publishing House. Before her marriage, Kirkie was on the staff of Young Life in Tacoma, Washington. She is a graduate of Wheaton College.

Acknowledgments

Thanks be to God, who by his power fulfills his purposes and brings into being all he prepared before the beginning of time! One of my greatest joys is seeing the Lord work! I thank him for his guidance in this study on prayer—for going before, preparing the way, directing and enabling as I wrote, and bringing this book into being. To him be the glory!

Also, I thank my dear husband, Terry, for his constant love, support, interest, and encouragement. He exemplifies Paul's admonition to husbands in Ephesians 5:25: "Husbands, love your wives, just as Christ loved the church and gave himself up for her." I thank the Lord for him, and for the love God has given us for each other.

I wish to acknowledge Pam Heim's suggestion for a weekly method of praying for your family (see pages 128-129). Then, too, I sincerely thank the following special friends who labored with me in prayer for this book, and who graciously reviewed the studies, sharing their thoughts and offering suggestions: Cathy Cheek, Bonnie Frum, and Jennifer Page. I would also like to thank Nancy Metz for her faithful commitment of prayer support, which I consider a gift from the Lord!

Introduction

Communication is important to us today. The time in which we are living has been called the "Golden Age of Communication." This need to communicate with one another across town and around our world has captured our imaginations. Increased attention has been given to the potential of electronics in communication industries, resulting in telephone innovations, home computers, and satellites in space, to name a few developments. Seminars are being conducted and books written on the art of interpersonal communication.

We want to hear and be heard, to understand one another and be understood. As human beings we have a basic need to communicate. But where does this need come from? In the Bible we are told that we, as male and female, are created in the image of God (Genesis 1:27). Could it be that God himself desires to communicate?

In exploring the Scriptures for insight, we do discover that our God is one who communicates with us. From the very beginning of time we see this truth revealed in God's written word, the Bible. In Genesis 1:28 it is recorded that God immediately *talked* with Adam and Eve after he created them. He established a *relationship* with those he created in his image. This was the outworking of love, which was what motivated God to create us in the first place!

The prime evidence of God's heart to communicate with us is seen in his act of becoming one of us in the person of Jesus Christ. "In the beginning was the Word, and the Word was with God, and the Word was God. . . . The Word became flesh and lived for a while among us" (John 1:1-14). The apostle Paul verifies this in Colossians 1:15—Jesus Christ "is the image of the invisible God." God actually took on flesh so we could know him! He walked on this earth and talked with people, revealing his heart, his plans, his desires. But does God just want to

7

communicate with us, or does he desire dialogue? Does he want us to talk with him as well?

Reuel Howe in *The Miracle of Dialogue* considers dialogue and its principles to be the basis of all effective communication. He describes "the principle of dialogue . . . as openness to the other side, with a willingness not only to speak but to respond to what we hear."[1] This is the kind of relationship we can have with God.

Throughout the Bible, the give-and-take nature of communication is illustrated. In the Old Testament, this is clearly seen in many conversations carried on between God and man. An example is the dialogue Abraham and God had regarding an heir for Abram, as he was then called (Genesis 15:1-5).

In the New Testament, Jesus not only conversed with his heavenly Father, but also taught us to go to God in prayer, expressing our heart to our Lord and hearing what he would say to us. Jesus' apostles, after Christ's ascension into heaven, actually dialogued with their risen Lord. (For example, see Acts 9:10-19.) In the letters they wrote to the various churches, the apostles continually exhorted the Christians to pray.

Scripture tells us that "Jesus Christ is the same yesterday and today and forever" (Hebrews 13:8). So we can believe that the Lord desires to communicate, to dialogue with us today. How exciting! What greater communication could one conceive of?

Yet prayer is often an enigma to us. "What good does it actually do to pray if God already knows anyway?" we might ask. "Is prayer anything more than an exercise we are required to do in performing as a good Christian?" "I hear about power in prayer, but my prayers only seem to get to the ceiling. Why?"

We all have questions about prayer. We long to experience in our own prayer lives the power spoken of in Scripture. We also desire to experience intimate dialogue with the Lord God! In knowing that this is God's heart as well, we can therefore approach this study with anticipation, claiming his promise to us in Matthew 7:7-8—"Ask and it will be given to you; seek and you will find; knock and the door will be opened to you. For everyone who asks receives; he who seeks finds; and to him who knocks, the door will be opened."

Note
1. *The Miracle of Dialogue* by Reuel L. Howe (The Seabury Press, 1963), page 40.

1
God's Invitation to You

Do you remember the childhood game played by picking the petals off a daisy to determine whether or not someone cared? "He loves me, he loves me not; he loves me, he loves me not; he loves me." Even if that last petal was "he loves me," you still could not be certain—for how dependable can daisy petals be?

Perhaps today that same uncertainty lurks in your subconscious mind regarding your God! So as we consider communicating with God— sharing ourselves with him and seeking the same from him—we need to examine the most important foundation of any intimate relationship, and that is *love*. If we are to be open and trusting in our relationship with him, it is crucial that we examine his heart toward us. We need to be assured that God truly does love us if we are to grow in our understanding and experience of prayer.

In the Bible God reveals his heart toward us. "For God so loved the world that he gave his one and only Son, that whoever believes in him shall not perish but have eternal life" (John 3:16). In Psalm 145:13 the truth is proclaimed that the Lord is "loving toward all he has made." We see God does love each of us! The depth and quality of this love is incomprehensible. Jesus gave us a glimpse of this depth though, when he said, "Greater love has no one than this, that one lay down his life for his friends. . . . I have called you friends" (John 15:13-15). Then he gave his life for the world he loved. This is the kind of love we hunger for! Paul expresses this phenomenal truth of God's uncon- ditional love for us in Romans 5:8—"God demonstrates his own love for us in this: While we were still sinners, Christ died for us."

Then with a burst of energy Jesus rose from the dead, conquering death once and for all! He was willing to pass through death, suffering the penalty of sin for our sakes, because he loves us. Now all who believe in him can experience a love relationship with him for eternity! With this assurance of God's love as the foundation for our study on prayer, let's turn to his word and explore further the invitation he extends to us.

God Bids Us Come

1. Read Isaiah 1:18.

   a. Express in your own words the invitation extended by the Lord.

   _____

   _____

   _____

   b. What kind of relationship does the Lord desire?

   _____

   _____

   _____

2. Read Isaiah 55:1-3.

   a. On what basis of merit, if any, is this invitation extended?

   _____

   _____

   _____

   b. What encouragement does this give you?

   _____

   _____

   _____

3. You may still have difficulty believing that God really is *for* you. This can adversely affect your attitude toward prayer.

   a. Examine what the Bible reveals and summarize the truth taught in each of the following passages:

Jeremiah 24:6 _____

_____

_____

_____

Matthew 7:9-11 _____

_____

_____

_____

_____

John 10:10 _____

_____

_____

_____

Romans 8:31-32 _____

_____

_____

_____

b. Describe your reaction to these verses.

_____

_____

_____

_____

c. Review these verses daily, talking with the Lord about them, asking him to cause these truths to take root in your heart.

4. What assurance does the truth expressed in Hebrews 13:8 give you?

_____

_____

_____

_____

God Tells Us to Pray

5. What should characterize our relationship with God, according to the following verses:

John 16:24 _____

_____

_____

Romans 12:12 _____

_____

_____

Philippians 4:6-7 _____

_____

_____

Colossians 4:2 _____

_____

_____

6. What does it mean to you that God is asking you to pray?

_____

_____

_____

_____

7. Read Acts 13:22.

   a. How does David describe himself in Psalm 109:4?

   _____

   _____

   b. What insight does this give you into God's commendation of David in Acts?

   _____

   _____

   _____

   _____

8. Turn to 1 Corinthians 1:9.

   a. As Christians, what have we been called into?

   _____

   _____

   _____

   b. Refer to a dictionary for a definition of fellowship.

   _____

   _____

   _____

   c. What do you usually think of as the primary emphasis in your relationship with God?

   _____

   _____

   _____

   d. How does the fact that the basis of our relationship with God is love explain his desire for fellowship with us?

   _____

   _____

   _____

   _____

   _____

NOTE

God Promises to Meet Us as We Pray

9. In the following verses, what is God's promise to us?

Psalm 91:15 _____

_____

Psalm 145:18-19 _____

_____

_____

Jeremiah 33:3 _____

_____

James 4:8 _____

_____

10. Read Hosea 6:3.

a. What promise is given?

_____

_____

_____

b. What is it compared to?

_____

_____

_____

c. How certain are those events?

_____

_____

11. Read Psalm 5:3. What should be our attitude as we go to the Lord?

_____

_____

_____

12. How is his nature described in Psalm 89:1-2?

_____

_____

13. What truth regarding God's faithfulness to his promises is stated in each of the following verses:

Numbers 23:19 _____

_____

_____

Nehemiah 9:8 _____

_____

_____

Hebrews 10:23 _____

_____

_____

16

14. Based on your responses to questions twelve and thirteen, what confidence can be yours each time you go to the Lord in prayer?

_____

_____

_____

_____

_____

SCRIPTURE MEMORY: Memorize James 4:8, or another verse you choose from this lesson.

QUESTIONS: Write out any questions you have at this point and bring them before the Lord, claiming Matthew 7:7-8.

_____

_____

_____

_____

_____

_____

Guidelines for Group Discussion

As you come together for study and sharing, it is important to commit that time to the Lord. He is in your midst. Extend to one another the same courtesies and attitudes you would appreciate from them. Encourage honest responses and accept one another at whatever point each happens to be in his or her growth in the Lord. Remember, the work in another's life and conviction of truth comes from the Spirit. As you come together in the name of Christ, the Lord will work in significant ways, truly resulting in praise to his name.

The questions at the conclusion of each study are additional questions that can be used for review if you are doing this study on an individual basis. If you are in a group, they can be incorporated by your group leader in guiding the discussion for fuller understanding and application of those truths studied during the week. The questions in the lessons themselves should be discussed first as a basis for further discussion.

Introduction to the book (pages 7-8): What are your thoughts and feelings regarding the realization that God desires to communicate with *you?* Is this discovery new to you? Describe any difficulty you may have in believing this on a practical, daily level.

Question 1: In the Song of Solomon, sometimes interpreted as an allegory, God is symbolically portrayed as the "lover," and we as the "beloved." Read the second chapter, verses eight through ten. Describe the desire of the lover to be with his beloved, as portrayed by the actions and words recorded. As you do so, picture yourself as the beloved. What choice does the beloved have to make? What are some "walls" people can build to keep God at a distance in their lives?

Question 2: Do you accept the openness of God's invitation, or is it easy to think, *My actions haven't been pleasing to the Lord lately. After I improve I'll be more deserving of being heard and ministered to by him.* What words in verses two and three indicate God's desire to communicate with us?

Question 3: Consider Matthew 7:9-11. Which image do you hold of God; a father who will give you a stone, or bread? Where do you think our misconceptions of God come from? What are some things you can do to form an accurate understanding of his true nature and his heart toward you?

Jeremiah 29:11, John 15:11, and Romans 8:28 also express the truth of God's desire for us.

Question 5: Other verses that express God's desire to communicate with us are Matthew 6:6, Ephesians 6:18, and 1 Timothy 2:1-4.

Question 8: What other perspectives are there regarding the primary reason God establishes a relationship with us? What importance does the realization of God's desire for fellowship with you place on prayer?

As we communicate with the Lord, we do not need to be concerned about how we phrase our prayers. We can talk to him as to a friend, wherever and whenever we so desire. Rosalind Rinker, in her book *Communicating Love Through Prayer* says, "If prayer is talking to Jesus, why not stop *trying to pray* and just talk to him? . . . He loves us no matter what we do, or how we pray."[1] Are you as comfortable talking with Jesus as you are with your best friend? Why, or why not?

Question 9: What do these promises mean to you, verse by verse, or as a whole?

Question 10: In Malachi 4:2 the Lord refers to himself as "the sun of righteousness." What fact do you know regarding the presence of our earth's sun, regardless of whether or not we can actually see it or feel its warmth on a particular day? What does that say to you regarding God's presence with you?

Questions 9 and 10: What is the value of consciously claiming these truths each time we go to him in prayer?

Question 12: How does 1 John 1:5 support this truth? What does this realization mean to you as you read God's word?

Lesson: How will you try to change your prayer life as a result of what you've discovered in this lesson?

Conclusion: Close with prayer.

Note
1. *Communicating Love Through Prayer* by Rosalind Rinker (Zondervan, 1966), page 62.

2
The Power of Prayer

There is awesome power in prayer. Through prayer, God's power is released to work mightily within and through us, bringing us to the fullness of our potential in Christ and releasing us to accomplish God's purposes in this world. When we pray, we are on holy ground!

In this lesson we will examine the reality of this power, and in the chapters to come we will discover how we can actually experience this power in our own prayer lives.

God's Power at Work In Us and Through Us

1. Read Ephesians 3:20-21.

   a. What does Paul say the Lord is able to do in and through us?

   _____

   _____

   _____

   b. How is God able to do this?

   _____

   _____

   _____

c. Who is the one to be glorified in this?

_____

2. These truths are expressed in 2 Corinthians 4:7.

   a. How does Paul describe the channels of God's power (you and me)?

_____

_____

_____

   b. Why has God given us this appearance?

_____

_____

_____

3. Read Paul's prayer in Ephesians 3:14-19.

   a. What does he pray the Christians will be filled with?

_____

_____

   b. What must take place first?

_____

_____

_____

_____

c. What insight does this give you regarding experiencing God's power in your life?

_____

_____

_____

_____

4. As we open our hearts to God, his Spirit will work through us in individual lives and in our world. Describe what God did through the following people:

David in 1 Samuel 17:32, 45-50 _____

_____

_____

_____

Elijah in 1 Kings 17:7-24 _____

_____

_____

_____

_____

Jesus' disciples in Mark 6:7-13 _____

_____

_____

_____

Paul and Barnabas in Acts 14:3 _____

_____

_____

_____

5. Read 1 Corinthians 2:3-5.

   a. How did Paul describe himself?

   _____

   _____

   _____

   b. What was the source of Paul's effectiveness in preaching about Jesus Christ?

   _____

   _____

   _____

   c. What was the result of Paul's preaching?

   _____

   _____

6. How does Paul describe God's kingdom as seen on earth? Read 1 Corinthians 4:20.

   _____

   _____

   _____

The Power of Individual Prayer

7. What fact is stated regarding prayer in James 5:16?

_____

_____

_____

8. The power of prayer is exhibited throughout Scripture. From the following passages identify the person who prayed and tell what happened as a result of his prayer.

Joshua 10:12-14 _____

_____

_____

_____

Judges 15:16, 18-19 _____

_____

_____

_____

1 Kings 18:22-39 _____

_____

_____

_____

_____

2 Kings 20:9-11 _____

_____

_____

_____

Acts 9:36-41 _____

_____

_____

_____

9. Read James 5:17-18.

   a. What description does it give of Elijah?

   _____

   _____

   b. What happened as a result of his prayers?

   _____

   _____

   _____

   c. What does this teach regarding the potential of God's power being manifested in your prayers?

   _____

   _____

   _____

Power in Group Prayer

10. As Christians gathered together for prayer in the days of the early church, God's power was released. What happened in Acts 12:5-14?

_____

_____

_____

_____

11. In Matthew 18:19-20, what is the key Christ gives us to powerful group prayer?

_____

_____

_____

12. Agreeing together is so important for effective group prayer! What insight does Philippians 2:1-2 give you about it?

_____

_____

_____

_____

13. Read Ephesians 6:18 and Jude 20. How are we to pray? How does this apply to questions 11 and 12?

_____

_____

_____

27

14. Group prayer can be a fearful experience for those unaccustomed to praying out loud. As God pours out his Spirit on us, what can we claim and depend on according to 2 Timothy 1:7?

_____

_____

_____

SCRIPTURE MEMORY: Memorize James 5:16, or another verse you choose from this lesson.

QUESTIONS: _____

_____

_____

_____

_____

_____

Guidelines for Group Discussion

Question 1: Can you relate an experience when you saw God answer a prayer of yours in a way that completely surpassed your expectation? Can you think of a current request that you could change to see more of God's unlimited power?

Question 3: What must be within our being before we can receive God's power?

Questions 1-3: According to Philippians 2:13, what will God accomplish through us? *His good pleasure*

Question 4: What does it mean to you that the power that accomplished these works lives in you? Can you relate any experience in which you saw God manifest his power in you, through you, or around you?

Question 5: What understanding does Paul's experience give you of Jesus' words in John 15:5? Do you think people generally rely on God's power, yielding to him; or do you think Christians often feel they need to do something for God? What is it important for us to do?

Questions 11-13: Can you recall a time when you experienced this agreement in the Spirit? What was the result?

Questions 11 and 12: Can you recall a time when you experienced this agreement in the Spirit? What was the result?

Question 14: What are some benefits of group prayer? What are some personal experiences or suggestions that might help all participate comfortably? Who are we praying to, and how can that thought free us from anxiety?

Because anxiety about praying in groups is common, don't call on anyone to pray unless you check with that person beforehand. When prayer is opened up to all who would like to pray, sentence prayers make it easier for all to participate. These are simple statements offered according to topic—a group conversation with the Lord. Allow time for silences, praying as the Spirit urges. An example follows.

"Thank you, Lord, for your presence here with us."

"Thank you for your promise to hear us and meet us now as we pray."

"Father, we hold Jim up before you as he undergoes surgery tomorrow. Please give him your peace as he anticipates this and enters the hospital today."

"Do guide the surgeons' hands as they operate. Give them your wisdom, knowledge, skill, and discernment."

"Be with Jim's family as they wait to learn of the results, comforting and strengthening them by your Spirit."

"May your name be glorified and your good purposes be accomplished in and through this situation."

Conclusion: Close by praying sentence prayers as illustrated above.

3
Essential Ingredients

When you think of prayer, do you think mainly of making your requests known to God Almighty?

Is prayer more than that? In any personal relationship, does intimacy involve more than making one's petitions known? Think of one whom you love. Isn't a natural part of that relationship affirmation of the other person, praising his good qualities? Do you say, "I'm sorry," and confess your mistakes when you have wronged the one you love? Do you thank him for gifts, for acts of kindness and thoughtfulness, for being a faithful, loving friend? Does that relationship involve listening while he shares what is on his heart? Do you simply enjoy being in one another's presence?

As you keep these thoughts in mind, turn to God's word to consider the elements that should comprise our dialogue with the Lord.

One Approach

1. When the disciples asked Jesus to teach them to pray, he gave them a model, recorded for us in Luke 11:1-4. Read this prayer and then decide whether each verse is an expression of adoration, confession, or a request (supplication).

    Verse 2 _____

    _____

    Verse 3 _____

    _____

31

Verse 4 _____

_____

2. David expresses his heart to the Lord in Psalm 19. For each element of prayer, list the verses that illustrate it.

Humility or Devotion —
Adoration _____

_____

Confession _*(circled mark)*_____

_____

Thanksgiving _*1 PRAISe*_____

_____

Supplication _____

_____

3. It is helpful whenever we spend time in prayer to first prepare ourselves by reading God's word. For each aspect listed below, read at least one selection, using the others for another time. Then write what you would pray based on each passage you read.

Adoration: 1 Chronicles 29:10-13; Psalm 100 or 139; Revelation 5:11-12

_____

_____

_____

_____

_____

Confession: Daniel 9:3-10; Psalm 32 or 51 _____

_____

_____

_____

_____

Thanksgiving: Psalm 16, 23, or 118 _____

_____

_____

_____

_____

Petition: Psalm 27, 63:1-8, or 86 _____

_____

_____

_____

_____

Intercession: 1 Chronicles 29:18-19; Psalm 20:1-5; Ephesians 1:15-19

_COMPASSION for other 101_____

_____

_____

_____

4. Praying for others (intercessory prayer) can be an opportunity for ministry.

   a. Read Exodus 17:8-13 and 32:7-14. How did Moses intercede for the Israelites in each situation?

   _____

   _____

   _____

   _____

   _____

   _____

   b. What difference do you see in the way each situation had developed?

   _____

   _____

   _____

   _____

   c. What are two general ways we can intercede for an individual or a group of people in prayer?

   _____

   _____

   _____

   _____

The Importance of Listening

5. In addition to speaking, there is another very important element
   in our communication with the Lord. Identify what this is by writing
   the key phrase from each verse below.

   1 Samuel 3:10 _____

   _____

   Psalm 85:8 _____

   _____

   Ecclesiastes 5:1 _____

   _____

6. What does God promise to do for those who listen?

   Proverbs 1:23 _____

   _____

   _____

   _____

   Jeremiah 33:3 _____

   _____

   _____

   Amos 4:13 _____

   _____

   _____

7. According to Proverbs 2:6 and James 1:5, why is it important for us to listen to God?

_____

_____

_____

_____

8. Read John 18:37-38. What tragic mistake did Pilate make in concluding his dialogue with Jesus?

_____

_____

_____

Recognizing His Voice

9. Jesus gives us insight into this dimension of our relationship with him in John 10:3-5.

a. What is important for the sheep (Christians) to do?

_____

_____

_____

b. Why are the sheep able to follow the shepherd?

_____

_____

_____

c. How do you learn to recognize another person's voice?

_____

_____

d. How can you learn to recognize the voice of the Lord?

_____

_____

_____

10. The Lord has provided a means through which we can know him, and through which he can speak to us.

a. Read 2 Timothy 3:15-16 to identify this means.

_____

b. In trying to discern God's voice through Scripture, wait for his Spirit to impress his words upon your spirit. Look up the word *quicken* in a dictionary. How does the Lord quicken our spirit when he is speaking to us?

_____

_____

_____

11. Read Elijah's experience as recorded in 1 Kings 19:11-13. What does the form of God's communication with Elijah teach you regarding listening?

_____

_____

_____

meditation

12. One tool in hearing God speak to us is meditating on him, a beauti
ful dimension of our prayer life.

a. Write Galatians 2:20 on a card you can carry with you. Think
about it during the next few days, asking the Lord to reveal
himself and give you insight about its meaning and application.
Record the thoughts that come to mind.

_____

_____

_____

_____

b. What did David meditate on, according to Psalm 143:5?

_____

_____

c. One way of using Scripture for meditation is to place yourself
in a biblical scene, using your imagination. However, before
meditating on the Lord in this way, it is important to pray for
God's protection so that nothing will touch you other than his
very presence. Find a quiet spot when you are not pressed for
time. Quiet your heart and your mind with prayer and God's
word. Then express your desire to meet with him in a time
of meditation.

For example, you might read John 11:17-32. After reading the
passage, imagine you are Mary. Picture yourself at home with
friends reflecting on thoughts deep within yourself. Your sister
comes in, touches you, and says, "Jesus is asking for you." You
go out to a pleasant, peaceful spot where Jesus is waiting. When
you see him, you are overwhelmed with his glory and his love,
and you fall down before him. Perhaps you feel his hands on
your arms, gently lifting you up, and he takes you in his arms
and holds you. You express to him your feelings and thoughts.

Now listen quietly and allow God to minister to you.

SCRIPTURE MEMORY: Memorize Luke 11:2-4, or another verse or passage from this lesson.

QUESTIONS: _____

_____

_____

_____

_____

_____

_____

Guidelines for Group Discussion

Question 1: In communicating with the Lord, one way to remember the key elements of prayer is the acronym *ACTS*.

A = Adoration;	praising and thanking God for who he is. This "sacrifice of praise" (Hebrews 13:15) delights his heart.
C = Confession;	repenting of our sins and asking his forgiveness.
T = Thanksgiving;	for the specific things he has done for us and through us, and for his blessings.
S = Supplication;	praying for the needs of others (intercession) and asking for ourselves (petition).

What are some examples of each element? Do you have a hard time separating praise from thanksgiving as you pray?

Question 2: Do you find that your prayers are mainly "asking" prayers, or do you include a balance of all the elements? Why is it important to include each one?

Question 3: Is it necessary to go through all these steps every time we want to speak to the Lord? For insight, consider Peter's prayer in Matthew 14:25-30.

Question 4: Do you have any difficulty seeing prayer as a real ministry? Do you sense the excitement of actually participating in a significant way in all that God desires to do in this world? How does the realization of the ministry of intercession affect your attitude toward prayer?

Question 5: Why is it important to listen to God? What are some of the difficulties you may encounter as you attempt to do this?

Question 8: Identify those influences that often can cause us to make the same mistake Pilate did.

Question 9: What do you mean when you say, "I heard his voice"?

Question 10: Read Psalm 119:97-105. What can you gain from God's word? What dangers are involved in haphazardly flipping through the Bible to find a verse you hope is from the Lord?

Question 11: Can you give an example of a time when the Lord has given you wisdom, encouragement, or direction as you "listened" to him?

Question 12: What personal experiences have you had during times of meditating on the Lord? What other Scripture passages could you use for an encounter with the Lord?

Conclusion: As a group, offer sentence prayers using each element of ACTS for direction.

4
The Quality of Honesty

Honesty is an extremely important quality if we desire intimacy in our relationship with the Lord, and if we long to experience a powerful prayer life as well!

The necessity of honesty for intimacy is true in any relationship. If someone we are close to is not being completely honest about what he or she is really feeling or thinking, it prevents us from being to that person what he or she needs. This presents a real hindrance to meaningful dialogue or relating on any significant level.

In our communication with the Lord, it is the same. If we are not honest with him, we do not allow him to minister to us where we really are. We begin to play games with him and intimacy falters.

When we are honest, we allow him to be all he desires to be to us! We grant him permission to meet us in our innermost self. There are no walls or pretenses. Intimacy deepens, and our prayers are truly effective.

For insight about honesty with the Lord, let's turn to his word.

God Wants Us to be Honest with Him

1. In Luke 18:9-14 Jesus relates the parable of the Pharisee and the tax collector. Who does Jesus commend, and why?

   _____

   _____

   _____

   _____

2. According to Psalm 145:18, what must we do to be confident that God hears us?

_____

_____

_____

3. What kind of worshippers does God the Father seek? Read John 4:23.

_____

_____

_____

4. Would God know if we weren't being completely honest about how we're thinking and feeling, and what we're doing?

_____

   a. Write the phrases from the following passages that reveal the extent of God's knowledge of us.

   1 Chronicles 28:9 _____

   _____

   Psalm 44:20-21 _____

   _____

   Psalm 139:1-4 _____

   _____

   Jeremiah 17:10 _____

   _____

b. What do these passages reveal to you regarding God's knowledge and understanding of your heart and mind right now?

_____

_____

_____

c. List those things you presently are doing, thinking, or feeling and about which you have not been completely honest with God.

_____

_____

_____

_____

God's Response to Our Honesty

5. As we do express feelings to the Lord that we may consider unacceptable, or come to him acutely aware of our weaknesses and unworthiness, we may wonder what his response will be to us (perhaps having experienced rejection in some relationship in the past).

a. It may be helpful to recall what he did for us when we were his enemies, as recorded in Psalm 65:3.

_____

_____

b. As Jesus was dying, as he had been tortured and spit upon by his enemies, as he was being mocked and ridiculed, what did he say in Luke 23:34?

_____

_____

6. Write the phrases from the following verses that express the nature of God's love.

Psalm 73:21-24 _____

_____

Psalm 86:5 _____

_____

Jeremiah 31:3 _____

_____

2 Timothy 2:13 _____

_____

7. The truth of these Scriptures is underscored in the experience of Kind David, recorded in Psalm 32. He had committed adultery with Bathsheba and then arranged to have her husband killed.

a. What was David doing in his relationship with the Lord?

_____

_____

b. How did he change his behavior?

_____

_____

c. What was God's response to David?

_____

_____

d. What confidence does this give you in going to the Lord?

_____

_____

_____

8. Read Jeremiah 20:7-18.

a. Describe Jeremiah's attitude toward the Lord and his feelings about his life.

_____

_____

_____

_____

b. What action does the Lord take toward Jeremiah?

_____

_____

_____

c. What encouragement does Jeremiah's experience give you to be honest with the Lord about whatever you're feeling?

_____

_____

_____

_____

Problems in Praying

9. There perhaps are times that we may not "feel" like praying, when we find ourselves withdrawing, "building walls," keeping God at a distance. Does the Lord know when we are feeling this way? Write out a verse or passage studied in this lesson that answers that question for you.

_____

_____

_____

_____

10. What step should we take when we are feeling this way?

_____

_____

11. We don't need to pray with words if our feelings are too deep to even verbalize.

a. How do we receive help at times like this, according to Romans 8:26-27?

_____

_____

_____

b. How did David react to such a time in his life? Read Psalm 77:4-12.

_____

_____

_____

12. Sometimes the Lord does not reveal any details to us in how to pray specifically for a person or about a situation. Our prayers are still effective if we honestly express our heart's desire to the Lord—the "bottom line," so to speak, in what we desire; or the result we long to see. So many times we concentrate on the *means*, rather than praying for the *end* and allowing God in his wisdom to work out the most effective means. Instead, we should wait and watch with anticipation to see the ways in which God will work. This is a powerful way to pray!

a. How does Paul illustrate this truth in his prayer for the Israelites, recorded in Romans 10:1?

_____

_____

_____

b. Record your heart's desire for each person closest to you, and for any unanswered requests you've been praying about.

_____

_____

_____

_____

_____

_____

_____

_____

_____

_____

Jesus' Response to Honesty

13. Examine the incident in Thomas' life recorded in John 20:24-28. What was the result of being honest about his doubts?

_____

_____

_____

14. The death of Jesus' good friend Lazarus is recorded in John 11. Read verses seventeen through forty-four.

    a. How would you describe Mary's response to Jesus?

    _____

    _____

    _____

    b. How did Jesus respond to her, and what did he do?

    _____

    _____

    _____

15. In John 4:7-26 Jesus converses with a woman who has been living a very promiscuous life. What was his response to her honesty?

_____

_____

_____

_____

16. Are you struggling with doubt or anger or sin, or something else that you need to be honest about with the Lord? Express what is on your mind.

SCRIPTURE MEMORY: Memorize Psalm 51:6, or another verse or passage from this lesson.

QUESTIONS: Review the questions you recorded in lessons one through three and write down any insights you have gained up to this point.

_____

_____

_____

_____

_____

_____

Guidelines for Group Discussion

Question 2: What may have to follow a prayer that is honest?

Question 4: Read Psalm 139:1-16, and list the kinds of things God knows about us. How does this awareness of God's complete knowledge and understanding free you to be totally honest with him? Can you share an experience when this truth enabled you to come before the Lord in all honesty? Have you let it make a difference in your walk with the Lord today?

In preparation for effective petitions, carefully examine your heart before the Lord. If there is something in your life that you know is not right, yet you really do not want to give it up, ask God to help you *want* to change your attitude. When the prayer is answered, *then* ask the Lord for strength not to do it.

Can you give an example or an experience illustrating this?

Question 5: God was willing to die for us while we were his enemies. (Also see Romans 5:8 and Ephesians 2:4-9.) How does that realization free you to be honest with him in prayer?

Question 6: How do these verses encourage you to be completely honest with the Lord? How does God's holiness affect your willingness to be honest?

Question 10: What advantages are there in being honest with the Lord when you don't feel like talking with him? If you don't know the reasons why you are feeling this way, ask God to reveal to you what those reasons are; and then ask him to minister to you in them. Can you share a personal experience when you did not feel like praying and what you learned that might be helpful to others?

Conclusion: Take time now to pray as a group or individually. Be very honest with the Lord about your feelings, desires, and actions—knowing that he is aware of the truth and wants us to come to him just as we are. His love for us is unconditional, and his grace is ministered to us freely as we come to him without pretense.

5
The Necessity of Surrender

Adamant; demanding; resistant; defensive.

Humble; seeking; receptive; yielding.

If a child or friend comes to you with a request, which of the two types of attitudes described above will encourage a positive response from you?

Often in our relationship with the Lord, we can become a whining, demanding, arrogant child, bent on having our own way. Our intention may not be to come across like that; we're only aware of how important something is to us.

However, changing our words and manner with the Lord is not the most important concern. What matters is our attitude of *heart!* As this changes, so does the effectiveness of our prayers because we can better know his will, be open to his mind, and pray accordingly with power, in his name. God can produce this change of attitude in us if we ask him to do so.

For insight into the attitude of heart God desires as we come to him, and what this involves, let's turn again to his word.

What God Asks

1. In Romans 6:13 and 12:1 what are we asked to do?

_____

_____

_____

_____

2. Read Romans 7:21-23. Why do we often experience a struggle in surrendering to God's answers to prayer?

_____

_____

_____

3. Does this mean that our will and God's will are always in opposition to each other? For insight, consider the incident in Joshua 5:13-15.

   a. What question did Joshua ask the Lord?

   _____

   _____

   b. What common approach to prayer does this illustrate?

   _____

   _____

   _____

   c. What does Christ's reply mean to you?

   _____

   _____

   _____

   d. Read Joshua 2:1 and 6:2. Did Joshua's will coincide or conflict with God's will concerning Jericho?

   _____

   _____

54

The Struggle of Self-Surrender

4. Often the concept of self-surrender can have negative connotations to us that present subtle barriers. To identify what we actually believe about surrender, read the statements given below. Mark each one true or false according to your first feeling.

   To me surrender means:
   a. always having to do what I do not want to do.   T   F
   b. accepting a "no" when I ask for something good or fun.   T   F
   c. being open to what God plans for me, realizing that
      he always knows what's best for me.   T   F
   d. being willing to receive a "yes," "no," or "wait"
      answer to my prayer.   T   F
   e. waiting, perhaps for a long time, with anticipation
      and expectation for God to act.   T   F

5. Often our difficulty in yielding comes from a misunderstanding of God—what he is really like and what he desires for us.

   a. From the following verses, write the phrase describing his heart towards you.

   Psalm 103:5 _____

   _____

   John 3:16 _____

   _____

   John 15:9 _____

   _____

   Ephesians 2:4-5 _____

   _____

   _____

The nature of his plan for you

Proverbs 2:7-9 _____

_____

_____

_____

Isaiah 48:17 _____

_____

_____

_____

Jeremiah 29:11 _____

_____

_____

John 10:10 _____

_____

_____

b. How do these truths help you yield to the Lord?

_____

_____

_____

_____

c. Ask God to free you from any fears you have that might prevent you from wholly surrendering yourself to him. Write out Christ's promise in John 8:32.

_____

_____

_____

_____

6. To yield to the Lord is not something we do only once! It is a continual process, and sometimes a very difficult one. For insight, examine Christ's experience in the Garden of Gethsemane recorded in Matthew 26:36-46. Describe Christ's struggle to surrender as he faced the cross.

_____

_____

_____

_____

The Help Available in Our Struggle

7. Read Hebrews 4:15-16.

a. What is the temptation we are studying in this week's lesson?

_____

_____

_____

_____

b. What is true about Jesus' temptations, as compared with ours?

_____

_____

_____

_____

c. How successful was he in handling them?

_____

_____

_____

d. When we are tempted, what should we do, and what will we receive?

_____

_____

_____

_____

8. According to Ezekiel 36:27 and Philippians 2:13, who changes our heart and enables us to surrender? What requests did David make of the Lord in Psalm 51:10 and 12?

_____

_____

_____

_____

9. As we yield to the Spirit who is at work within us, what are the results as indicated by Paul in Romans 8:5-6?

_____

_____

_____

10. Summarize what our responsibility is in our struggle for self-surrender and the help that is available to us.

_____

_____

_____

_____

11. As an expression of praise, write out 1 Corinthians 15:57.

_____

_____

_____

Personal Application

12. The Lord knows us intimately and desires honesty in our relationship with him. List those areas in which you are having the greatest difficulty yielding to the Lord, or a person or a situation that is hard for you to release to him.

_____

_____

_____

13. Now talk with the Lord about each one, being honest about your struggle to surrender. Then ask him for his help in yielding (or *wanting* to yield) to his will. In submitting, you become a team working together for his good purposes.

14. In closing, write out the benediction in Hebrews 13:20-21.

_____

_____

_____

_____

SCRIPTURE MEMORY: Memorize Romans 12:1 or another verse or passage from this lesson.

QUESTIONS: _____

_____

_____

_____

_____

_____

_____

Guidelines for Group Discussion

Question 1: What does this mean in our daily concerns? What is the opposite attitude or approach? How is it a hindrance to an effective prayer life?

Lloyd J. Ogilvie comments on this attitude in prayer: "Prayer becomes our efforts to get the Lord to march to the demanding drummer of our self-will . . . We call in the reserves of his strength for our battles."[1]

Question 2: How often do you struggle to surrender in your everyday life, from the little concerns to the biggest decisions? From personal experience, can you describe the effect within when you resist yielding your will to the Lord? Contrast that with the results of genuine surrender.

Question 4: Statements c, d, and e exemplify the attitude of surrender God desires in us as we come to him. Did you detect any conflict between your feelings and what you actually know to be true? If so, why do you think this happens?

Question 5: What other truths have you discovered about God, or experiences have you had, that help in yielding to the Lord?

Question 6: What lessons from Jesus' experience can we apply to our own life?

Question 7: What are some common areas of struggle we all face today?

Question 10: Why is this an important realization for you?

Conclusion: Read Hebrews 13:20-21, followed by a time of group prayer.

Note
1. *When God First Thought of You* by Lloyd J. Ogilvie (Word Books, 1978), page 168.

Faith - a moral & spiritual
   quality of an individual by
   virtue of which man has
   confidence in God (& fidelity
   to Him)
Faith is intellectual & moral!
   Belief in the truth God reveals &
      then the
willingness to be guided by # truth

dict - confidence or trust in a
         person a thing - Belief
         which is not based on proof
_____

Trust - Dict.
   Reliance on the integrity,
strength, ability, surety of a
person or thing ; hope

6
The Dynamics of Faith and Trust

There is an element of guilt that can be unintentionally imposed by well-meaning Christians when they say, "Your prayer would be answered if you only had more faith." So we work hard at trying to produce a strong enough *feeling* of faith in order to earn our answer to prayer. If it appears to be unanswered, we take upon ourselves the responsibility for that, consequently becoming consumed with guilt.

What actually is faith, and what part does it play in unleashing God's power? Are answers really earned by how much faith we can muster; or does faith come from God himself for a certain purpose of his? How does trust fit into all this?

One often hears or says, "Simply trust God," or "Just have faith." Are trust and faith one and the same? At times they are used interchangeably. Yet in studying God's word we discover some important differences, as well as a significant relationship between the two.

These are all important questions for discovering real power in prayer. Ask the Lord to open your eyes to his truth as you now turn to his word.

The Importance of Trust

1. As we have considered the importance of being honest with our Lord and have examined the necessity of surrendering ourselves to God for his will, we have discovered that there is an element that enables us to do so.

   a. Read Psalm 62:8 and identify what we are asked to do at all times. How does this enable us to pour out our hearts to God?

   Pour out your heart to [it]

   Trust and

63

_____

_____

_____

_____

b. What truths in Psalm 37:5-6 and Proverbs 3:5-6 enable us to
surrender in trust?

Commit your way to the Lord

_____

_____

_____

2. What word in Psalm 84:12 and Proverbs 16:20 describes the man
who trusts in the Lord?

Blessed is man who trust *happy* *pleased*

3. Write a dictionary definition of the word *trust*.

_____

_____

_____

4. Describe David's trust in God as revealed in Psalm 13.

_____

_____

_____

_____

5. What are some reasons why trust is an important quality in prayer?

_____

_____

_____

_____

_____

_____

Developing Trust

6. In any relationship, the better we get to know someone, the more *Note* we discover whether or not that person can be trusted. God's word helps develop our trust in him. What attributes are ascribed to him in the following verses:

Psalm 36:5-9 _____

_____

Psalm 63:2 _____

_____

Psalm 111:7 _____

_____

7. Read David's words recorded in Psalm 22:1-5. What is David doing to develop trust in God?

_____

_____

_____

65

8. What is recorded in Luke 8:38-39 and Acts 15:4 that is another means of developing trust?

_____

_____

_____

_____

9. 1 Chronicles 5:20 indicates another way to develop trust in the Lord. What is it?

_____

_____

_____

Faith

10. Faith is defined in Hebrews 11:1. Write a definition of faith based on that verse.

_____

_____

_____

11. Explain why trust provides a springboard for faith.

_____

_____

_____

_____

66

12. Which do you find personally influences your faith most of the time—facts or feelings?

_____

13. Which one provides the firmer, more stable foundation, and why?

_____

_____

_____

_____

The Source of Our Faith   *How*

14. Write the phrases from Acts 3:16 and Romans 12:3 that indicate how we obtain our faith.

_____

_____

_____

15. According to Mark 9:24 and Luke 11:13, what should we do as we desire for God to increase our faith?

_____

_____

_____

16. Read Hebrews 12:2. Who nurtures our faith, or causes it to grow?

_____

_____

Action Faith

17. Describe the faith spoken of in Matthew 21:22.

_____

_____

_____

_____

18. This faith becomes active in at least three ways. One of the most significant is _listening_ to the Lord. He gives us insight as to his purpose in a given situation, thereby directing us in how to pray.

   a. Read John 16:13 and Ephesians 5:18. How does the Holy Spirit become involved in helping us apply our faith?

   _____

   _____

   _____

   _____

   b. What difference in action do you see between the people listed in Hebrews 11:7-11 and those in Ezekiel 13:3 and 6?

   _____

   _____

   _____

   _____

   _____

c. What promise does the Lord give in Isaiah 44:26 about the prompting of the Holy Spirit?

_____

_____

_____

19. For what individuals, situations, or decisions would you like to receive insight from the Lord regarding how to pray?

_____

_____

_____

_____

20. A second way action <u>faith is manifested</u> is by actions or words based on what we know the character of God to be. We delight him by our faith, which he therefore honors. In Matthew 8:5-13 and Hebrews 11:23, what incidents illustrate this faith?

NOTE

_____

_____

_____

_____

21. The character of God is revealed in Psalm 111. What words of praise are used by the psalmist to describe the Lord?

_____

_____

_____

22. From what you know about the Lord, write a brief prayer or psalm of praise.

_____

_____

_____

_____

_____

23. A third way action-faith is manifested is through the Holy Spirit directing our words.

   a. How could Elijah's experience in 1 Kings 18:20-39 be an example of this?

   _____

   _____

   _____

   _____

   b. Can you recall a time the Holy Spirit directed your words?

   _____

   _____

   _____

   _____

   _____

24. Prayers of faith are responses to what the Lord says through the Holy Spirit, and what we know about God's character. What does this mean in terms of working up an emotion of faith and then demanding that God comply?

_____

_____

_____

_____

SCRIPTURE MEMORY: Memorize Hebrews 11:1, or another verse or passage from this lesson.

QUESTIONS: _____

_____

_____

_____

_____

_____

_____

Guidelines for Group Discussion

Question 3: What role does trust play in an intimate relationship?

Question 4: Why is trust like that of David a necessity in our relationship with God? As you examine your own walk with the Lord today, are you able to say, whatever the circumstances are or become, "Lord, I trust you"?

Question 9: Can you share an experience in which stepping out in trust resulted in greater trust?

Question 10: Why do you think it's true that faith applies to what we hope for and what we do not see? Explain the difference between trust and faith.

Question 13: What are some ways your factual foundation for faith can be strengthened? What fact concerning God does each group of verses teach:

    a. Psalm 65:3; John 3:16; Romans 5:8; Ephesians 1 and 2; 2 Timothy 1:9-10.
    b. Isaiah 53:5-11; Romans 3:21-25; Romans 8:1; 1 John 1:9.
    c. Joshua 1:5; Psalm 73:23; Isaiah 16:5, 41:9,10,13, 43:1-5; Romans 8:31-39.
    d. Psalm 12:6, 18:30; Isaiah 40:8; Mark 13:31.

Are there any other facts which you have discovered in these lessons thus far that are meaningful to you? What personal experiences have you had when your feelings would have, or did, affect your faith?

Question 16: God's word can increase our faith. In what other ways can we give him opportunities to nurture this faith in us?

Question 18: In Jeremiah 23:16 and 18, what does the Lord say is critical? How can you do this in prayer?

Question 24: Andrew Murray understood that "it is not *faith* that heals, but faith is the hand that *receives* the gift from the *Healer,* who is God."[1] Therefore our faith is not power over God! Rather, in believing God to be who he is, we enable him to do what he intends, for only he knows what is best. We become a *channel, bringing his power* to a situation. This is a very important truth to grasp! List those points studied in this lesson that verify this truth.

Conclusion: Close with group prayer.

Note
1. *Andrew Murray: Apostle of Abiding Love* by Leona Choy (Fort Washington, Pennsylvania: Christian Literature Crusade, 1978), page 152.

7
Hindrances to Effective Prayer

"You are a garden fountain,
a well of flowing water
streaming down from Lebanon."

Thus the lover praises his beloved in Song of Solomon (Song of Songs) 4:15.

In considering the analogy of flowing water, we know that it is possible for everyone to have running water in his home today. The resource and necessary knowledge are available. Water meets a basic need for life. It also can be harnessed to produce power.

In our relationship with the Lord, prayer provides a channel for God's power to flow into our lives. Like water, prayer meets a basic need for our spiritual life, and can be harnessed to provide power.

To actually have water in our homes we must tap the main water supply. Even then pipes can become plugged up or break, and our water supply dwindles or stops altogether. The channel is no longer open for the water to flow freely, with full power, into our homes.

These facts are analogous to our relationship with the Lord and contain some truths critical to our understanding of effective prayer. We have already considered the hindrances of a lack of honesty and a lack of surrender. For insight into some other significant hindrances to effective prayer, let's open God's word, praying for true openness to him as we do so.

Not Having Christ Within

1. What hindrance to effective prayer is pointed out in John 6:35-36?

_____

_____

_____

_____

2. Read John 4:4-14 and 7:37-38.

   a. If we want the water of life, what must we do?

   _____

   _____

   _____

   b. What is God's promise to us if we do this?

   _____

   _____

   _____

3. What will we become, as described in Romans 8:15-17 and 1 Peter 2:9-10?

   _____

   _____

   _____

4. Being related to God and filled with living water are gifts from him. According to 1 John 5:11-12, who receives them?

   _____

   _____

   _____

5. If you have not already asked Christ to come into your life, but would like to do so, simply ask him in your own words. Express your heart to the Savior now. He loves you and longs to live within you, giving you life now and forevermore.

_____

_____

_____

_____

_____

_____

6. What will God do about his promises for those who are his children? Read 2 Corinthians 1:20.

_____

_____

7. Explain the hindrance that not being in God's family presents to an effective prayer life.

_____

_____

_____

_____

_____

Sin

8. Once a relationship has been established, fellowship begins. The relationship is secure, regardless of our behavior; yet fellowship

can be impaired. Read Psalm 66:18 and Isaiah 59:2.

a. What can clog the channel of our life with Christ, restricting free-flowing fellowship with him?

_____

_____

_____

b. What insight does the word *cherish* (Psalm 66:18, NIV) give you?

_____

_____

_____

9. What is the effect of sin on our prayers? Read James 4:3.

_____

_____

_____

10. The truth of how sin deadens our sensitivity to the Lord, and even results in a change in our nature, is dramatically portrayed by David.

a. Read 2 Samuel 11:1-5 and 14. Describe his sin with Bathsheba and his sin against Uriah.

_____

_____

_____

_____

b. David had a very intimate relationship with the Lord in which he listened readily to discern what he was saying to him, and yet the Lord had to send his prophet Nathan to confront David regarding his sin (2 Samuel 12:1). Why do you think that was necessary?

_____

_____

_____

_____

11. Read David's prayer in Psalm 139:23-24 as your own, opening yourself to God's light. Record whatever he brings to your mind.

_____

_____

_____

_____

_____

_____

12. What was David's response after Nathan confronted him with his sin? Read 2 Samuel 12:13.

_____

_____

_____

13. After David acknowledged his sin, he wrote Psalm 51. Write the phrases that express

his confession _____

_____

_____

_____

his requests _____

_____

_____

_____

14. Read the following verses to find what attitude God desires for us to have toward our sin.

Psalm 51:17 _____

_____

_____

Joel 2:12-13 _____

_____

_____

2 Corinthians 7:10 _____

_____

_____

15. In Proverbs 28:13 and 1 John 1:9, what does God *promise* to do for us as we confess our sin to him?

_____

_____

_____

16. It is a fact that we are forgiven and cleansed if we confess our sin. What must we do if we don't feel forgiven?

_____

_____

_____

_____

17. Confessed sins are all in the past—even those we confessed just today. In Philippians 3:13-14 what does Paul say we should do now?

_____

_____

_____

_____

18. Read Proverbs 1:23 to see why confessing our sins opens the way for effective prayer.

_____

_____

_____

19. If we confess our sin, what will the result be within us, as expressed in Psalm 32:1-5?

_____

_____

_____

_____

Satan's Opposition

20. A third hindrance to effective prayer is illustrated by an experience that Daniel had. Read Daniel 10:2-14.

   a. How much time lapsed from when Daniel prayed until his prayer was answered?

   _____

   b. Describe the struggle that took place during that time.

   _____

   _____

   _____

   _____

   c. What can take place today in the spiritual realm when we make a request of our Lord?

   _____

   _____

   _____

   _____

21. Read 1 Peter 5:8-9.

    a. Who is our enemy?

    _____

    b. Describe Satan's behavior.

    _____

    _____

    _____

22. What truth is proclaimed in Colossians 2:15 and 1 John 4:4?

_____

_____

_____

_____

_____

23. What does God provide for our protection in this battle, as listed in Ephesians 6:13-18, and what weapons are available for our use?

_____

_____

_____

_____

_____

_____

24. In 2 Corinthians 10:4-5, what does Paul claim our divine weapons can do?

_____

_____

_____

_____

25. How does the admonition in Ephesians 6:10 apply to opposing Satan?

_____

_____

_____

_____

26. In lessons four, five, and seven you have studied the following hindrances to effective prayer: lack of honesty, lack of surrender, not being a Christian, unconfessed sin, and Satan's opposition. Ask the Lord to reveal to you any of these hindrances that may be affecting your prayer life. Write down any insights he gives you now or in the days ahead.

_____

_____

_____

_____

_____

_____

SCRIPTURE MEMORY: Memorize 1 John 1:9 or another verse or passage from this lesson.

QUESTIONS: _____

_____

_____

_____

_____

_____

Guidelines for Group Discussion

Question 3: Read John 3:3-6. What phrase indicates how a person becomes a child of God?

Question 4: What does Paul mean in Galatians 2:20?

Question 5: Have someone pretend to not be a Christian and ask some questions regarding how he or she could become a child of God. Let the group respond to that person, to help him establish a relationship with God. Remember the importance of loving and accepting the individual!

Question 8: We all battle sin continually in our lives. Does that mean God will never be free to answer our requests? Can you recall an example of what cherishing sin in our lives can do?

Question 9: The extent of how fellowship can be damaged by sin is seen in the book of Lamentations. The writer laments how God's people have given in to sin and no longer walk closely with the Lord. What results does he record in Lamentations 2:9?

Question 10: What do David's actions say to you regarding temptation in your own life? From your own life or the life of another, can you describe the change that takes place within a person who is cherishing sin in their life?

Question 12: What other responses might David, or any of us, have had?

Question 14: Do you think repentance involves a long grieving process in which we weep and mourn our sin; or instantaneous remorse of the heart, during which we immediately confess and receive forgiveness; or both?

Question 15: What words in 1 John 1:9 reveal that we can count on God to do what he says? How does Jesus illustrate what he does for us in Zechariah 3:1-4 and John 13:2-9?

Question 17: What does this mean about letting guilt from the past bog us down in our life for Christ today?

Question 19: Read Psalm 103. What is David expressing in verses ten through twelve? Review those things you wrote down in question eleven. Write each one on a separate piece of paper. Confess them, tear the paper up, and throw it away! Then claim God's total forgiveness for each one—to be remembered no more!

Question 21: Is Satan on the offense or defense? What should your reaction be to that fact?

Paul E. Billheimer in *Destined for the Throne* explains why we sometimes need to keep asking and asking. He writes that "Satan never allows an answer to reach earth if he can prevent it. Persistence and importunity in prayer are not needed to persuade a willing God but to enable him to overcome opposition of hindering evil spirits. . . . This is the reason for the biblical teaching on the importance of importunity."[1]

Is Satan's interference a new realization for you? What are your reactions to this discovery? Because these forces are unseen, do you have difficulty believing they actually exist and do battle against us today? What are you praying for now that might illustrate this struggle?

Question 22: What confidence and encouragement does this give you as you battle Satan through prayer?

Question 23: How can this armor become yours? Can you give an illustration of a time when you used this armor and what resulted?

Question 24: How does this realization affect your desire to spend time in prayer?

Conclusion: If you did not do so earlier, read aloud Psalm 103 as an expression of praise to the Lord. Then conclude with group prayer.

Note
1. *Destined for the Throne* by Paul E. Billheimer (Fort Washington, Pennsylvania: Christian Literature Crusade, 1975), page 108.

8
The Key to Powerful Prayer

Jesus tells us in John 14:13, "I will do whatever you ask in my name, so that the Son may bring glory to the Father."

What enables us to pray in the power of the name of Jesus, thereby bringing glory to God? We all long to understand this. The beautiful truth is that God wants us to know! He gave us the privilege of prayer so we can dialogue with him. He has commissioned us to go and bear fruit in this world for him. He wants us to be effective in prayer!

There are two dimensions to prayer. One occurs in special times apart with him as well as in continually walking through our day with him. Our dialogue is spontaneous and free, as conversation normally is with one to whom we are especially close. Each of us enjoys a unique relationship with him since he created us to be unique.

The other dimension occurs when power is released through prayer with exciting, observable results such as when Isaiah prayed and the sun's shadow moved back ten steps (2 Kings 20:9-11).

Both dimensions are a natural, integral part of our communion with the Lord. He wants us to experience the fullness of both, so ask him now to reveal to you his truth regarding powerful, effective prayer. Remember his promise: "Ask and it will be given to you; seek and you will find; knock and the door will be opened to you. For *everyone* who asks receives; he who seeks finds; and to him who knocks, the door will be opened" (Matthew 7:7-8).

Remain in Christ

1. In John 15:7 we read, "If you remain in me and my words remain in you, ask whatever you wish, and it will be given you." What

89

phrases do you think reveal the key to dynamic prayer?

_____

_____

_____

2. Read the preceding verses in chapter fifteen. What insight do they give about what it means to remain in Christ?

_____

_____

_____

_____

3. What is the key to powerful prayer, and what does this mean for you on a daily basis?

_____

_____

_____

_____

4. How is it possible for a person to be a true Christian and live with Christ daily, yet not abide in him?

_____

_____

_____

_____

5. Reflect for a moment on your own walk with the Lord. Are you abiding in Christ most of the time? If not, honestly express your feelings regarding this and any fears or apprehension you might have.

_____

_____

_____

_____

6. In lesson seven we studied the importance of confessing our sins, thereby experiencing God's cleansing. We can understand this truth by visualizing a reservoir full of stagnant water. Christ refers to himself as "the living water." As the clean spring water pours into this reservoir, the old water spills out, until only fresh spring water remains. We are filled with Christ; he abides in us.

How is being cleansed and then filled with Christ described in Romans 13:12-14 and Ephesians 4:22-24?

_____

_____

_____

_____

_____

7. Identify the means Jesus used to remain in the Father as recorded in Luke 5:16 and 6:12.

_____

_____

_____

8. Write the phrase in Romans 12:12 that exhorts us to pray, and explain what it means.

_____

_____

_____

_____

9. An example of how prayer keeps us in the Father and he in us is seen in Acts 4:31. Describe what the believers were doing, how they were affected, and what the result was.

_____

_____

_____

_____

_____

10. According to John 6:56, what is another means of remaining in Christ?

_____

_____

_____

11. a. What are we told to do in Colossians 3:1-2?

_____

_____

b. What are some things that compete for your attention—that which you set your heart, mind, and eyes on?

_____

_____

_____

_____

c. The focus of our attention that God desires for us is summarized in Hebrews 3:1 and 12:2. What is it?

_____

_____

_____

Let Christ's Words Remain in You

12. According to Ezra 7:6, 9-10, and 25, what did Ezra saturate himself with? What results did he exhibit in his life because of it?

_____

_____

_____

_____

13. What does the word accomplish in our lives, as recorded in John 17:17, and what does this mean?

_____

_____

_____

93

14. It is so very important to *saturate* ourselves in God's word—to read it, study it, meditate on it, memorize it! As we spend time in the Scriptures, our focus is established on him and we can more easily discern his voice; we are remaining in him and he in us! Examine your life. How much time do you spend in God's word? In what ways have you seen him use his word in your life? What resolution would you like to make regarding the reading of his word?

_____

_____

_____

_____

_____

_____

God's Promise

15. Read John 15:7-8.

   a. What is God's promise to us?

   _____

   _____

   b. Because it is God himself doing his work in us and through us, who is therefore glorified?

   _____

   c. Read verses four through eight, using your name throughout this key passage, as though Jesus was speaking directly to you. (for so he is!).

SCRIPTURE MEMORY: Memorize John 15:7 or another verse or passage from this lesson.

QUESTIONS: _____

_____

_____

_____

_____

_____

Guidelines for Group Discussion

Introduction: What are some differences between the two dimensions of prayer?

Question 1: What phrases are used in other translations for the idea of remaining in Christ?

Question 2: J. Dwight Pentecost writes, "Think of the relation of a branch to a vine. You cannot tell where the stalk of the vine leaves off and the branch begins, because the branch and the vine are in vital union. They are one, not two. The life that is in the stalk flows through the branches. There are not two lives, one life for the stalk and another for the branch. There is only one life, shared together by the branch and the vine."[1]

Question 4: What is the difference between living your life for Christ and Christ living his life through you?

Question 5: What differences do you notice in yourself when you are not abiding as opposed to those times when you are?

Question 6: Why is cleansing so important if we are to remain in him? What happens if we knowingly permit sin in our lives rather than being honest with God about it? How will this affect our prayer life?

Question 10: How can we "feed on Christ" each day, apart from the sacrament of communion? What are the differences and similarities in the communion services of the churches represented in this group?

Question 11: In the Song of Solomon 1:15 the lover, representing the Lord, delights in his beloved for she has eyes like a dove. A dove has single vision, only being able to focus on one thing at a time. How does this apply to us? Should we ignore everything else around us? What should be the practical outworking of this day by day? What insight about abiding do you get from Matthew 6:22?

Actually, our focus cannot even be abiding, for then it shifts from the person of Christ to a state, or an experience. Just as fellowship is a natural by-product of believers coming together, so abiding is a natural result of keeping our focus on the Lord and resting in him.

We can get some understanding of abiding in *Hudson Taylor's Spiritual Secret* by Dr. and Mrs. Howard Taylor. We are not to *strive* to abide, but to *rest* in Christ! He is everything and as we yield to him and rest in him, *his life flows through us!* Taylor calls this key to abiding the "exchanged life."

Question 14: According to 2 Timothy 3:15-17, what ways can the Lord use Scripture in our life?

Conclusion: Close with prayer.

Note
1. *The Glory of God* by J. Dwight Pentecost (Multnomah Press, 1978), page 102.

9
Results of Remaining

If we remain in Christ and he in us, the results are obvious in ourselves and our experiences. It's exciting! God is free to be the God he claims to be and desires to be in us! We experience the abundant life Jesus said he came to give (John 10:10). We are filled with his joy. Following his discourse on remaining in him (John 15:1-10), Jesus says, "I have told you this so that my joy may be in you and that your joy may be complete." As this becomes real in our experience, we can say with the psalmist, "But as for me, it is good to be near God" (Psalm 73:28).

Let us examine some of the results we experience as we remain in our Lord Jesus Christ, particularly as they apply to dynamic prayer.

Manifesting the Fruit of the Spirit

1. Read Galatians 2:20.

   a. Who actually *lives in* us?

   _____

   _____

   b. What does the verb *live* mean to you?

   _____

   _____

   _____

2. Read John 15:4-5. Explain what Jesus is saying about developing fruit of the spirit.

_____

_____

_____

_____

3. What words or phrases in Ephesians 3:16-19 make you think of the relationship of a branch to the vine?

_____

_____

_____

_____

4. As we remain in the Lord and he in us, specific qualities of his become part of us, as described in Galatians 5:22-23.

   a. What are they?

_____

_____

_____

_____

   b. Who do these qualities belong to?

_____

_____

5. Considering Galatians 3:3 and 2 Corinthians 3:18, how do these become a natural part of us?

_____

_____

_____

6. Read John 15:7. How does this truth of manifesting the person of Christ relate to effective prayer?

_____

_____

_____

_____

Having the Mind of Christ

7. You read in Galatians 2:20 that Christ lives in you. As he remains in you, what is yours as stated in 1 Corinthians 2:16?

_____

_____

8. Describe how this helps us in the following circumstances:

a. Counseling one in need

_____

_____

_____

_____

b. Discerning which of the many tasks before us God has for us to do

_____

_____

_____

_____

c. Understanding the root of confusing behavior in our spouse, child, friend, associate or someone else

_____

_____

_____

_____

d. Knowing how to pray

_____

_____

_____

_____

9. What element of prayer studied in chapter three is especially important in the above circumstances? Why?

_____

_____

_____

Using the Authority of the Name of Christ

10. By understanding the mind of God through the Spirit of Jesus Christ as we remain in him and he in us, we can pray in his name, according to his will. By so doing, God's power is unleashed! Underscore the phrases in the first sentence for question ten that state what is necessary to effectively use the name of Christ.

11. The power inherent in the name of Christ is clearly taught and exemplified throughout Scripture. For the following verses and passages, write the phrases that refer to the power of Christ's name, and describe the results.

John 17:11 _____

_____

_____

_____

Acts 4:7,10 _____

_____

_____

_____

_____

Acts 4:29-31 _____

_____

_____

_____

_____

Philippians 2:9-11 _____

_____

_____

_____

12. Consider the illustration of one in authority today. If the President
of the United States sent you on a mission, you would simply say
you came in his name and there would be results. Why does
Jesus Christ have even greater authority behind his name? Read
Colossians 1:15-20.

_____

_____

_____

_____

13. After reading each of the following verses, write the condition
God gives us for effective prayer and his promise.

John 15:16 _____

_____

_____

_____

John 16:23-24 _____

_____

_____

_____

1 John 5:14-15 _____

_____

_____

_____

14. Read Acts 3:12 and 16. What truth about power is emphasized?

_____

_____

_____

_____

15. As you paraphrase 2 Corinthians 4:7, include the truth about the power of Christ's name.

_____

_____

_____

_____

16. Talk now with the Lord about your own remaining in him. Share with him your desires, fears, frustrations, weaknesses, and expectations. Remember that he wants you to come to him, to abide in him. He understands your uniqueness, and he promises to draw near to you. In his grace he meets you where you are and receives you in his love.

_____

_____

_____

_____

_____

_____

SCRIPTURE MEMORY: Memorize 2 Corinthians 4:7 or another verse or passage you choose.

QUESTIONS: _____

_____

_____

_____

_____

_____

_____

Guidelines for Group Discussion

Question 1: What does it mean to you that Christ lives in you?

Question 5: What point does Paul underscore in Galatians 3:3? In the past have you assumed these qualities were traits you were responsible for incorporating into your behavior? How will you change your attitude and approach to them, if at all?

Question 9: Being sensitive to the mind of Christ (listening) helps us know when to persist in prayer regarding something specific and when not to continue praying. Francis Hunter in her book *Hot Line to Heaven* writes, "If you feel once is enough, great. If you feel a need or an urge to pray more than once for the same thing, then just keep on praying until you feel in your heart there is no further need to pray."[1]
Can you share an experience when you knew you no longer needed to pray about something, and a time when you felt the need to continue in prayer? What were the results in each case?

Question 10: In an article entitled "The Monk and the Cripple: Toward a Spirituality of Ministry," Henri J.M. Nouwen writes,

> Here we touch the mystery of ministry. Ministers are powerless people who have nothing to boast of except their weaknesses. But when the Lord whom they serve fills them with His blessing they will move mountains and change the hearts of people wherever they go. The best way to express this is with the biblical words: 'In the name.' Ministers are those who think, speak and act not in their own name, but in the name of their Lord . . .
>
> To live in the name of Jesus Christ means first of all to live in intimate communion with Jesus, and through Him with our divine Father . . . Yet only one thing is necessary: to keep our eyes on our Lord, to remain attentive to His will and to listen with care to His voice (Lk. 10:42). If it is true that only with, in and through Jesus Christ can our ministry bear fruit, then our first and only concern must be to live in ongoing communion with Him who has sent us out to witness in His name. . . . Prayer is the basis and the center of all our ministry.[2]

Question 12: Read other passages that reveal the authority of Jesus

Christ—Psalm 8; Isaiah 45:5, 18-22; John 1:1-3; Philippians 2:5-11; and Revelation 19:16.

Question 12: Can you recall an experience you had in which the power and authority of the name of Christ brought mighty results? What have we studied in earlier lessons that is essential for answered prayer?

Question 16: Remaining in Christ is the key not only to powerful prayer, but to the entire Christian life as well. How many results of abiding in Christ can you list from chapters eight and nine?

Conclusion: Close with group prayer.

Notes
1. *Hot Line to Heaven* by Frances G. Hunter (Warner Press, 1973), page 84.
2. "The Monk and the Cripple: Toward a Spirituality of Ministry" by Henri J.M. Nouwen, *America,* March 15, 1980, page 207.

10
The Value of Time

Time is one of our most precious commodities. Moses says in Psalm 90:12, "Teach us to number our days aright, that we may gain a heart of wisdom." Do you consider your days as gifts from the Lord and ask him how he would like you to spend the time he has given you? There are so many demands, pressures, and responsibilities in life that it's sometimes easiest to give your time to the "squeaky wheel," or whatever catches your attention first.

Setting priorities is one good way to discern how you should best spend your time. Pray for God's mind in discerning them and then write them down. Take a look at how you spend your time. Do your priorities and your practice coincide?

Since God has called you into fellowship with himself, he desires special times apart with you in which that relationship can be nurtured. If one of your priorities is to remain in him, time spent with God alone is essential. There aren't any shortcuts. A growing relationship takes time and effort. To maintain oneness in marriage, for example, time must be spent just with one another, so dreams can be shared, hurts bared, pressures discussed, and thoughts and feelings communicated. That's how we truly know one another.

If in all honesty you're really not sure you want to take time each day ιo be with the Lord, ask him first of all to give you the desire. Then ask him to give you the strength and self-discipline necessary to set time aside. Start with whatever amount of time you realistically can spend. God in his grace and love receives us whenever we come to him, for whatever amount of time. As we discover the value of times apart with him, he increases our desire to spend greater lengths of time with him, helping us remain in him. Let's consider God's word and some practical helps to better enable us to take that time.

The Example of Jesus

1. Describe the relationship Jesus had with his Father, as revealed in John 17:20-23.

_____

_____

_____

_____

2. What did Jesus do to nurture and maintain that relationship, and what additional effort was sometimes necessary?

   Matthew 14:22-23 _____

   _____

   _____

   _____

   _____

   Luke 4:42 _____

   _____

   _____

   _____

   Luke 6:12 _____

   _____

   _____

   _____

3. What implications does Jesus' example have for you in your relationship with the Lord?

_____

_____

_____

_____

The Rewards of Earnestness

4. Read Matthew 5:6.

   a. Describe the desire of the one who receives the blessing.

   _____

   _____

   _____

   b. Remembering that Jesus Christ is our righteousness (Jeremiah
   23:6), what is the promise given in Matthew 5:6?

   _____

   _____

   _____

   _____

5. Describe the intensity of desire portrayed in Psalm 84:2.

   _____

   _____

   _____

6. What instructions did David give to the Israelites, recorded in I Chronicles 22:19?

_____

_____

_____

7. In Hebrews 11:6, what is necessary regarding seeking God?

_____

_____

_____

_____

8. What does Jesus commend Mary for in Luke 10:38-42?

_____

_____

_____

_____

9. How would you describe your attitude toward knowing God better?

_____

_____

_____

_____

_____

10. What does God promise in Jeremiah 24:7?

_____

_____

_____

_____

A Time and Place

11. What block of time do you have almost every day that is not preceded and followed by responsibilities or pressures? Setting aside a period of time will allow the Lord time to get through the "layers" you come to him with (from the immediate concerns on your mind to the deep needs in your heart).

_____

_____

_____

12. Which day or evening during your week can you schedule a longer segment of time?

_____

13. What does God teach us in 1 Corinthians 10:13 that applies to spending time with the Lord? What is his promise?

_____

_____

_____

_____

_____

14. Identify specific obstacles of any kind (tangible or intangible) that are, or most likely will be, a hindrance to you personally in spending time with the Lord. List ways you can overcome each one.

_____

_____

_____

_____

_____

_____

15. Read Mark 1:35, Luke 5:16, and 6:12. Then describe the kind of place Jesus sought for his times with the Father.

_____

_____

_____

16. What place that is available to you best fits the description above?

_____

_____

Helpful Tips

17. In Psalm 95:6-7 what position before God is encouraged and why?

_____

_____

_____

18. It may be helpful to read God's word out loud. Hearing it as well as seeing it may help you retain it better. You may catch things you might have missed otherwise. Reading out loud also helps keep your mind from wandering.

19. It's also helpful to pray aloud to keep your mind on what you are doing. It also may increase your realization that you definitely have prayed about those things. That's a psychological help, for God hears us whether we speak out loud or only with our thoughts.

20. A prayer notebook is a helpful tool.

   a. Why do you think it might be meaningful to you to keep a notebook of your requests and God's answers?

   _____

   _____

   _____

   _____

   b. Read Psalm 77:7-12. How would a prayer notebook help in a time of discouragement?

   _____

   _____

   _____

   _____

   c. You could also record the thoughts, guidance, or insights received while talking with the Lord.

21. Lloyd J. Ogilvie in *The Bush Is Still Burning* writes, "Those who dare to persist in a habitual daily time of quiet solitude find resources for living nothing else can provide. Jeremiah said, 'I sat

alone, because Thy hand was upon me' (15:17). God lays his hand of blessing and power on us when we are quiet."

Ogilvie goes on to say, "Solitude is not for evasive talking to God, but for incisive listening. 'Be still, and know that I am God' (Psalm 46:10). 'In quietness . . . shall be your strength' (Isaiah 30:15)."

Then he quotes Arthur Rubenstein and says, "What Arthur Rubenstein said of practice, I say of solitude: 'If I fail to practice one day, I know it; if I miss practicing two days, my agent knows it; if I refuse to practice three days, my public knows it.' And so with us in our relationships. If we have no solitude, we have nothing to give to people when we are with them."

Ogilvie concludes by saying, "Acquiring the Lord's attitude requires listening to his inner voice. We need a quiet time each day and then frequently during the day to see things from the Lord's perspective. Then we can ask him to take charge of things and show us how to act and react."[1]

SCRIPTURE MEMORY: Memorize Song of Solomon 2:10 or another verse or passage you choose.

QUESTIONS: _____

_____

_____

_____

_____

_____

_____

Guidelines for Group Discussion

Introduction: What are some priorities (both general and specific) that you live by now? What is a good way to evaluate them? How can you work the best priorities into your life day by day?

Question 1: Other verses that express the same truth are John 10:30; 14:9-10; and 14:20.

Question 2: Henri Nouwen writes how important it is to "be burning with love for the Lord" as we minister to others. "This requires a deep commitment to contemplative prayer in which we enter into our closet and spend 'useless time' with our Lord and him alone."[2]

Question 3: What kinds of thoughts and circumstances might have distracted Jesus' attention from his relationship with his Father? How do the pressures and circumstances of your life compare with his?

Question 4: Why do you think the phrase *hunger and thirst* is used? What difference, if any, might there be between hungering and thirsting for righteousness?

Question 5: Psalm 42:1-2 and 63:1 also reveal a strong desire for God's presence.

Question 6: What could the statement about the sanctuary refer to in a symbolic way?

Question 7: According to Matthew 6:5-6, how should we pray in order to receive God's reward?

Question 10: Can you share a time when you earnestly sought God—to know him better or for insight and guidance or for encouragement or for some other need. How did he meet your need?

Question 11: What time of day is best for you, and why?

Question 14: In the Song of Solomon 2:15 (Song of Songs) what could "the little foxes" be that keep Christians from spending time apart with the Lord, thus ruining the fruit being produced?

117

What obstacles are you presently struggling to overcome? Can you share some ways in which you have eliminated some obstacles in your life? One way to overcome an obstacle may be to visualize Jesus eagerly waiting for you where you regularly spend time with him. You might also memorize Song of Solomon 2:10 (Song of Songs) and repeat it whenever an obstacle of some sort presents itself.

Question 16: Is it good for you to have a regular spot to go to? Why?

Question 17: In what ways could this position be helpful?

Question 20: Some find it helpful to write out their entire prayers. What do you think the benefits might be? If you are already keeping a prayer notebook or journal, can you share an experience in which it was very meaningful or useful to you?

Conclusion: Read Isaiah 40:30-31. How might waiting on the Lord apply to the subject of this lesson? What results might we experience as we do this? Close with group sentence prayer.

Notes
1. *The Bush Is Still Burning* by Lloyd J. Ogilvie (Word Books, 1980), pages 165, 166, and 100.
2. "The Monk and the Cripple: Toward a Spirituality of Ministry" by Henri J. M. Nouwen, *America,* March 15, 1980, page 208.

11
Methods of Prayer

Variety is the spice of life, including our prayer life! Being in a rut can produce boredom and cause interest to wane. Variety in our times apart with the Lord not only keeps us feeling alive as we pray, but it also helps us expand the range of our prayers, bringing God's power to so many more individuals and situations.

One method for prayer was studied in chapter three, using *ACTS* to help you remember the various elements to incorporate in your prayers (adoration, confession, thanksgiving, and supplication, along with listening). In this chapter let's consider and use some other methods which are helpful in expanding your prayer life.

Scripture as a Springboard

1. So often we keep reading the Bible and prayer separate. Integrating them, using whatever passage we are reading as a springboard for prayer, is an exciting way to pray! As God's words form the essence of our prayers, we *know* we are praying in accordance with his will.

    a. Consider Colossians 3:1-7. Use each phrase or verse as a springboard for prayer. If you wish, use the lines below to write your prayer for each phrase or verse.

    _____

    _____

    _____

_____

_____

_____

_____

_____

b. Reflect on your expression to the Lord. Which elements in the ACTS method did you use?

_____

_____

_____

Topical Prayer

2. There are a variety of methods for supplication, of which topical prayer is one. Read Colossians 1:3-12 and list the things that Paul prayed for people.

_____

_____

_____

_____

3. Pray for at least one individual who is on your heart in each of the following groups:

a. Those you desire to come to know the Lord

_____

b. Those you long to see grow in the Lord, to hunger after him, to walk closely with him

_____

c. Those seeking God's direction in their lives

_____

d. Those experiencing problems in a relationship

_____

e. Those who are sick

_____

f. Those who are lonely

_____

g. Those who are poor, or are in need in some way

_____

4. Write four of your own topics for prayer and the names of those who are on your heart for each.

_____

_____

_____

_____

_____

_____

Categorical Prayer

5. Philippians 1:3-11 is another example of how Paul prayed for others. What kinds of things in addition to those listed for question two are given here?

_____

_____

_____

_____

_____

6. Here is one possible way to categorize people you'd like to pray for. Take time now to pray for at least one person in each category.

Family
    Immediate _____

    Relations _____

Friends
    Past _____

    Present _____

Neighbors
    Past _____

    Present _____

Associates
    Business _____

    Church _____

    Hobby or recreation _____

7. Write some categories that are meaningful for you.

_____

_____

_____

_____

_____

_____

Praying by Areas

8. Read Matthew 28:16-20. Think of the parts of the country or world you have visited or lived in. Write the names of non-Christians you knew and pray for each of them.

_____

_____

_____

_____

9. Pray for Christians in those areas, but first write down six things to pray about.

_____

_____

_____

_____

_____

_____

_____

_____

_____

10. What are three things you should pray about for any nation in the world?

_____

_____

_____

_____

_____

11. Pick up a daily newspaper and write down three needs in your own community, across the country, or around the world.

_____

_____

_____

_____

_____

_____

Pray for those needs, as well as people God could call to meet them. Ask him for insight as to what you might do also.

Stream-of-Consciousness Prayer

12. Read 2 Timothy 1:3-9. What thoughts in this passage could be the basis for powerful prayer?

_____

_____

_____

_____

13. In stream-of-consciousness prayer, pray regarding whatever and whomever comes to your mind. Ask the Lord to bring to your thoughts those who are in need of prayer. Ask also for insight as to how to pray for them.

14. During the next few days be very alert for thoughts of people or circumstances about which you can pray. Jot them down as they come to mind. Pray about your own concerns as well.

_____

_____

_____

_____

_____

15. What other thoughts for prayer do you find in Ephesians 1:17-19?

_____

_____

_____

_____

16. Holding someone up before the Lord is similar to stream-of-consciousness prayer, but a greater amount of time is spent praying for specific individuals. For example, present someone close to you to the Lord, concentrating on keeping that person in his presence.

Ask for insight as to what he is feeling, and what his specific needs are.

Ask what you can do to help that person.

Ask how you can help that person develop his gifts.

Ask the Lord to give you his heart for that person.

Pray that you will find a special way to show your love today.

Pray that he would desire to know the Lord better.

Pray that he would realize God's love more fully and would love him with all his heart, mind, soul, and strength.

Pray for that person's future and for those who will play a significant part in it.

Creative Insights

17. What word would you use to describe Moses' conversation with God in Exodus 33:12-17?

_____

18. God is the most creative Being! He desires to impart his wisdom and understanding to us. It can be exciting to open your mind to him for creative approaches to your involvements and circumstances. List some of your relationships or responsibilities and situations, and ask God to give you his creative insights regarding ways to bring freshness, fun, meaningful touches, or new attitudes to each one. Write down the insights as he gives them to you.

_____

_____

_____

_____

_____

SCRIPTURE MEMORY: Memorize Philippians 1:9-11 or another verse or passage from this lesson.

QUESTIONS: _____

_____

_____

_____

_____

_____

_____

Guidelines for Group Discussion

Question 1: Apply the same method to an Old Testament portion, 2 Kings 17·33 and 39. How did you like incorporating prayer into your reading?

Question 4: What are some topics under which you could list some requests for yourself?

Question 7: What difference do you see between topical prayer and categorical prayer? In what way could they be used together?

Question 9: Prayer for Christians wherever they are should include the following requests: spiritual growth, strength in persecution, health and supply of their physical needs, discovery and use of their spiritual gifts, hearts that respond to God's call to meet the needs of the world.

Question 10: In *Destined for the Throne,* Paul Billheimer quotes S.D. Gordon: "Prayer puts one in touch with a planet. I can as really be touching hearts for God in far away India or China through prayer as though I were there. . . . A man may go aside today, and shut his door, and as really spend a half hour in India for God . . . as though he were there in person."[1]

Question 14: How did you react to these methods of prayer, either as a group or individually?

Question 16: Did you receive any insights or changed attitudes toward that person that you could share?

Question 18: What are some creative insights he has given you or someone you know concerning a marriage, children, a job, a ministry, or some other situation? Do you often think of the Lord as a resource person for creativity in relationships, circumstances, and tasks? What word or phrase comes to your mind first when you think of God answering prayer?

Are there other methods of prayer that you have found effective? What are they? You might use the following method to pray for your family day by day.

Monday—marriage relationship and mates for children

Tuesday—temperaments of each family member
Wednesday—wisdom from above for each person
Thursday—thanksgiving concerning each one
Friday—family relationships
Saturday—safety (physical, mental, emotional, spiritual)
Sunday—spiritual growth
If you have an area of concern on your heart, assign one aspect of it to each day of the week so that it will receive regular prayer.

Conclusion: Close with group prayer.

Note
1. *Destined for the Throne* by Paul Billheimer (Christian Literature Crusade, 1979), page 104.

12
The Glory of God

> Worthy is the Lamb, who was slain, to receive power and wealth and wisdom and strength and honor and glory and praise (Revelation 5:12).

> Who is he, this King of Glory?
> The Lord Almighty—
> he is the King of glory (Psalm 24:10).

God deserves to receive glory! He is a holy and awesome Lord. His splendor is magnificent. His power is immeasurable—it far surpasses comprehension. By merely giving the command, he created our world. The psalmist states, "The heavens declare the glory of God; the skies proclaim the work of his hands" (Psalm 19:1). By his power we are redeemed and given eternal life. By his power and in his wisdom he guides our steps through each day, leading us in that plan he has prepared.

Then there is his love! Jesus said, "Greater love has no one than this, that one lay down his life for his friends. . . . I have called you friends" (John 15:13-15). And then he gave his life for us. For him to have come to die, leaving his heavenly throne to take on our humanity, is a depth of love impossible to grasp. Then to take hold of our hand in love and walk with us in faithfulness through our days, promising to be with us always, is truly awesome. Such love reveals the very heart of God.

For these reasons and more, we say with the psalmist,

> "Not to us, O Lord, not to us
> but to your name be the glory,
> because of your love and faithfulness" (Psalm 115:1).

John White writes in *Daring to Draw Near,* "That as we mature

131

spiritually, our prayers will become theocentric, . . . God-centered . . . God's honor and reputation are subjects you should be praying about."[1] Therefore let's consider the glory of God!

God Is a God of Glory

1. God desires that we glorify him because he *is* a God of glory! What statement of this truth is given in each of the following verses:

   Psalm 96:8 _____

   _____

   _____

   Mark 13:26 _____

   _____

   _____

   John 2:11 _____

   _____

   _____

   Revelation 4:11 _____

   _____

   _____

2. We need to pray that God will receive the glory that is his—through our lives as well as this world. How did the psalmist make this request in the following Psalms:

   79:9 _____

   _____

142:7 _____

_____

_____

143:11-12 _____

_____

_____

3. Write your own prayer for the Lord to receive the glory that is his in our world and in our lives today.

_____

_____

_____

_____

_____

_____

4. Through what means does God desire to be glorified?

Ecclesiastes 3:14 _____

_____

_____

Isaiah 55:11-13 _____

_____

_____

John 15:8 _____

_____

_____

Ephesians 1:11-14 _____

_____

_____

5. Do you find that your motivation in life is to glorify God?

_____

In what ways are you doing that now?

_____

_____

_____

_____

How could it be a greater source of motivation for you in the future?

_____

_____

_____

_____

_____

_____

Glorify Him in Your Being

6. God is concerned with our being—who we are and how we reflect him. What is his goal for us, as expressed in 2 Corinthians 3:18?

_____

_____

_____

7. How does God desire our lives to glorify him? Read Philippians 1:11 and 2 Thessalonians 1:12.

_____

_____

_____

8. What understanding does this give you of the purpose of those hard times you sometimes experience?

Zechariah 13:9 _____

_____

_____

Titus 2:14 _____

_____

_____

Hebrews 12:10-11 _____

_____

_____

James 1:2-4 _____

_____

_____

1 Peter 1:6-7 _____

_____

_____

9. Talk with the Lord now regarding your desire to glorify him in what you are now and are becoming.

_____

_____

_____

_____

_____

Glorify Him in Your Doing

10. We are to glorify God in those tasks he gives us to do and needs he calls us to meet in his name. This is a natural outworking of our being, for if Christ is living in us, we have his heart, his mind, and his will to respond in a hurting world. In what specific ways can you glorify God through what you do?

Matthew 5:16 _____

_____

_____

_____

1 Peter 4:10-11 _____

_____

_____

_____

11. How are both aspects of glorifying God expressed in Hebrews 13:20-21?

_____

_____

_____

_____

12. Read Revelation 19:7. The bride of Christ is the body of believers. How can our being and our doing bring God glory at the wedding of the Lamb?

_____

_____

_____

_____

13. Identify some ways God is being glorified through the works of his servants today.

_____

_____

_____

_____

14. Examine your own life. Are you aware, perhaps through affirmation from others, of ways in which the Lord has been glorified through you? (If so, this should not be a matter of pride but of praise to him, for he accomplishes his purposes through us by his grace.)

_____

_____

_____

_____

Worship This God of Glory

15. The Lord designated the responsibilities of the Levites in 1 Chronicles 23:5 and 30. What was one of their duties?

_____

_____

_____

16. John White writes, "God should receive from you the worship that such a God merits."[2] How is that worship described in Psalm 95:6?

_____

_____

_____

_____

17. What are we to continually offer to God, stated in Hebrews 13:15?

_____

_____

18. As a means of worship and praise, prayerfully write the phrases from the following Psalms that glorify God.

43:4 _____

_____

_____

44:8 _____

_____

_____

86:12 _____

_____

_____

111:10 _____

_____

_____

138:2 _____

_____

_____

148:13 _____

_____

_____

_____

19. Read Romans 12:1. What constitutes our most meaningful worship?

_____

_____

_____

_____

What does this involve?

_____

_____

_____

20. As you conclude this study on prayer, express to the Lord your thoughts and desires about presenting yourself to him.

_____

_____

_____

_____

_____

_____

SCRIPTURE MEMORY: Memorize Psalm 115:1 or another verse or passage from this lesson.

QUESTIONS: Review your questions from the previous lessons, making note of insights you have received on each one.

Guidelines for Group Discussion

Introduction: In what ways, or for what reasons, do you see God as the King of Glory?

Question 1: Read the description of God's glory recorded in 1 Chronicles 29:10-13.

Question 2: Another example of how to pray, desiring God to be glorified, is in Daniel 9:17. What does he ask?

Question 4: According to James 4:2, why do we not have those things we desire? Keeping in mind the fact that God desires to be glorified, why do you think we need to ask for those things the Lord already knows we need?

Question 6: How is this goal expressed in Colossians 1:27, and Isaiah 60:21 and 61:3?

Question 7: What examples can you give of people who glorify God through their being?

Question 8: How does the awareness that God can use difficulty for your good help you during the difficult times?

Question 10: Why is God's first concern with our being?

Question 13: Read Matthew 5:14-16 and 6:1-4. These two passages seem to contradict each other. Can you reconcile them? Consider the aspect of motivation. In what spirit are we to do those things the Lord asks us to do?

Question 17: What does the phrase *a sacrifice of praise* mean?

Question 18: What are some other ways, perhaps rather unusual, in which we can worship God?

Question 19: Do you think this is a one-time decision or a life-time process? Why? According to Isaiah 56:6-7, what will the Lord do for those who offer themselves to his service?

Conclusion: What discoveries did you make regarding prayer during this study? In what ways have you been helped specifically in your prayer life? Did you make some discoveries regarding God himself through this study? Do you have any questions still on your mind about prayer? Read the doxology in Jude 24-25, and then close with a time of group prayer.

Notes
1. *Daring to Draw Near* by John White (Inter-Varsity Press, 1977), page 80.
2. Ibid., page 108.